MONEY MINDSET MAKEOVER

From Scarcity to Abundance: Overcoming Mental Barriers to Financial Success + Financial Literacy Basics

SUMMER YESIL

CONTENTS

Chapter I   01
The Power of Your Money Mindset

Chapter II   08
Unpacking Your Money Story

Chapter III   19
Building a Solid Financial Foundation

Chapter IV   26
Mastering the Art of Smart Investing

Chapter V   34
Scaling Your Investments and Creating Multiple Streams of Income

Chapter VI   42
Advanced Financial Planning Techniques

Chapter VII   51
Leveraging Financial Technology and Tools

Chapter VIII   60
Financial Education for Sustaining Success

Chapter IX   69
Strategies for Generational Wealth

Chapter X   78
Adapting to the Evolving Financial Landscape

Chapter 1: The Power of Your Money Mindset

My Story

Let me take you back to a time when my financial life was, to put it lightly, a hot mess express. I was buried in debt, working a job that drained my soul, and living paycheck to paycheck. Every unexpected bill or minor financial hiccup sent me into a panic. I remember thinking that if I could just make a little more money, everything would be okay. But no matter how much money came in, it never seemed to be enough.

Back then, I thought the problem was purely financial, but the truth is, it was all in my head. My mindset about money was rooted in scarcity and fear. I was constantly worried about not having enough, about losing what little I had, and about never being able to catch up. I saw money as something elusive, almost like a mythical creature—always just out of reach.

And I used to believe that a 9-5 job was the golden ticket to escaping my less-than-stellar reality. I was in the healthcare field, slogging through days that felt like an eternity, surrounded by coworkers who shared the same limited outlook on their careers and lives. We all seemed trapped in a cycle of scarcity and competition, clinging to the idea that doing well in school and securing a stable job was the only route to financial success and societal prestige. But then, I had a revelation: what if there was more to life than grinding away in a job I didn't enjoy? Once I challenged and shifted my subconscious belief that my only path was to work under someone else, everything began to change. New opportunities started presenting themselves, and I began to see business and investment ideas everywhere I looked. I was astounded to discover that many people were living their dream lives, enjoying financial abundance, and often without working tirelessly or at all. It was like I had been given a backstage pass to the world of possibilities, and I realized that my old beliefs had been nothing more than a self-imposed cage.

The turning point came when I started putting effort into analyzing and reprogramming my subconscious beliefs about money. This mental evolution started my financial evolution. It was only then when I decided to dip my toes into real estate investing. I bought my first rental property, and let me tell you, I was terrified. I was convinced something would go wrong—that the market would crash, that I'd lose all my savings, that my tenants would destroy the place. I was so caught up in my fear that I almost backed out. But I didn't, due to the work I had put in with changing my money beliefs, I held my investments and ignored any fear based thoughts. And that's when I learned my first big lesson about money: your mindset shapes your reality.

In the beginning, because I was so focused on everything that could go wrong, I started to see problems where there were none. I hesitated on decisions, second-guessed myself, and, not surprisingly, things didn't go smoothly. My negative mindset was manifesting in real, tangible ways. I wasn't attracting success; I was repelling it.

But then I had this epiphany—if I continued to see money as something to be feared, I would always live in fear. I realized that I had to change the way I thought about money if I wanted to change my financial situation. So, I made a conscious decision to flip the script. I started telling myself that there was more than enough money out there for me, that I was capable of attracting wealth, and that I deserved financial success.

Another mental shift I had to make was improving my financial literacy. Learning the ins and outs of how money works, how money is transferred, stored, made, etc. is the cornerstone of any successful journey toward financial freedom. Without a solid understanding of money management, even the best financial goals can fall apart. It's like trying to build a house without knowing how to use the tools—disaster is almost inevitable.

It wasn't easy, and it didn't happen overnight. Shifting your mindset is a bit like trying to teach a cat to do yoga—it takes time, patience, and a whole lot of effort. But once I started focusing on abundance rather than scarcity and started to learn about how money worked, things began to shift like magic. I began spotting opportunities where I once saw only obstacles. For example, in real estate, I began to spot undervalued properties that others overlooked. My newfound confidence led me to negotiate better deals and make smarter investments. My rental property portfolio grew, and so did my income.

But it didn't stop at real estate. With this new mindset, I ventured into stock investing and even started a couple of businesses. The more I practiced abundance thinking, the more my wealth grew. I began to understand that money is just a tool—a resource that, when managed with the right mindset, can open doors to limitless possibilities.

Looking back, the most significant shift wasn't in my bank account, but in my mind. I moved from a mindset of scarcity and fear to one of abundance and opportunity. And that's what I want to share with you in this book. If you believe that money is hard to get, that it's scarce, and that you're not worthy of financial success, then that's exactly what you'll experience. But if you can start to see money as something abundant, as something you're fully capable of attracting and managing, then your entire financial life will begin to transform.

This is the foundation of everything we'll discuss in this book. Your money mindset is where it all begins. It's the lens through which you see every financial decision, every opportunity, and every challenge. And just like I did, you can shift that mindset to create the financial success you've always dreamed of. So, let's dive in and start reshaping how you think about money. Believe me, if I could do it, so can you.

My Transformation

Once I had made the decision to shift my mindset from scarcity to abundance, the results were nothing short of transformative.

One of the first things I noticed was a newfound clarity and focus. With my old scarcity mindset, I was constantly worried about what could go wrong and many times I didn't try new ways of making money because I just assumed it would fail. But as I embraced an abundant and financially literate mindset, I started seeing opportunities everywhere. I remember launching my first Etsy shop and instead of fixating on the potential risks—like whether anyone would actually buy my products—I began envisioning all the possibilities. What could my shop become? How could it grow and reach more customers? This shift from a fear-based approach to an opportunity-focused one allowed me to make decisions with confidence and creativity. By focusing on opportunities rather than obstacles, I began to see the potential for growth. Instead of fearing failure, I saw each challenge as a chance to improve and innovate. My shop began to thrive, generating more sales and positive feedback than I initially anticipated.

Another remarkable change was how my interactions with others evolved. Operating from a mindset of abundance naturally drew in like-minded individuals who also saw money as a positive force. Networking became not only more enjoyable but also incredibly productive. I found myself connecting with mentors and peers who were supportive and shared my new outlook. These relationships opened doors to invaluable insights and opportunities that would have remained closed if I had stayed in my old, fear-based bubble. Previously, my relationships were clouded by jealousy, competition, and gossip—low-vibrational energies that drained me. But as I transformed my inner world, my outer world started reflecting that change, attracting the right people and elevating my entire network. Even the activities I shared with friends shifted dramatically; where once my weekends were filled with clubbing, raving, and chasing fleeting highs, my circle now spends our time working out together, brainstorming business ideas, exchanging insightful podcasts, and other high vibe activities.

One of the most profound changes was in how I dealt with setbacks. In the past, financial challenges felt like insurmountable obstacles. Now, they were simply part of the journey—opportunities to learn and grow. When faced with a setback, I approached it with curiosity rather than dread. What lessons could I extract from this experience? How could I use this to improve my strategy? This mindset shift made navigating the ups and downs of financial life much easier and less stressful.

The transformation wasn't instant, and it certainly wasn't easy. It required consistent effort and a willingness to challenge deeply ingrained beliefs. But as I embraced an abundance mindset, I found that not only did my financial situation improve, but my overall quality of life did too. I was more confident, more proactive, and more optimistic about the future.

So here's the takeaway: your money mindset is the foundation of your financial success. If you're operating from a place of scarcity and fear, you're likely limiting your own potential. Similarly, if you're trying to build wealth without mastering the basics—like how to save, where to invest, or how to protect your assets—you're setting yourself up for failure. True financial success requires both the know-how and the strategy to make your money work for you. And if you can shift to a mindset of abundance and possibility, you'll open yourself up to new opportunities and experiences that can lead to remarkable success. This chapter is just the beginning of that journey. Using this book, learn to embrace the power of a positive money mindset, and watch how it transforms your financial reality.

Chapter 2: Unpacking Your Money Story

Our financial mindset is often shaped by a complex web of influences, including our childhood experiences, cultural beliefs, and societal expectations. These elements form what I like to call our "money story"—a narrative that guides how we perceive and handle money throughout our lives. In this chapter, we'll delve into how to unpack and understand your money story, so you can start rewriting it for financial success.

Think back to your early interactions with money. What were you taught about it? What messages did you receive from your parents, teachers, or media? For many of us, our money story begins with the lessons we learned as children. Perhaps you were told that money doesn't grow on trees or that it's a source of stress and conflict. These early messages often embed themselves deep within our psyche, shaping our beliefs about money.

Consider my own experience growing up. My parents were poor immigrants from Vietnam, frugal to a fault, believing that spending money was akin to wasting it. They instilled in me a strong belief that financial security was only for those who scrimped and saved meticulously. While their intentions were good, this mindset led me to approach money with a sense of scarcity and fear. I believed that if I spent money on anything other than necessities, I was being irresponsible.

Cultural beliefs and societal expectations also play a significant role in shaping our money story. For instance, societal messages often glorify wealth and success, while simultaneously stigmatizing those who struggle financially. This can create a dichotomy where wealth is seen as a mark of personal success and poverty is viewed as a personal failure. These messages can deeply influence how we view our own financial situation and our potential for financial success.

Another common societal belief is the belief that "Rich people are bad". You cannot become rich yourself if you subconsciously think that wanting money and having money is a negative thing.

Many people, including myself in the past, harbor a subconscious belief that wealthy individuals are inherently "bad" or morally questionable. This belief is often shaped by societal narratives that portray rich people as greedy, corrupt, or disconnected from the struggles of ordinary people. Such stereotypes can be perpetuated by media portrayals, cultural attitudes, and even personal experiences. This negative association can create a barrier to financial success, as it subconsciously discourages us from aspiring to wealth or pursuing financial opportunities. Recognizing and addressing this bias is crucial for shifting our mindset towards viewing wealth as a tool for positive impact and personal growth rather than a marker of moral failure.

Contrary to the negative stereotypes, wealthy individuals and successful businesses can have a profoundly positive impact on society. Many rich people use their resources to support charitable causes, fund innovative projects, and create opportunities for others. Businesses, at their core, are systems designed to address needs and solve problems, providing value to customers and communities. The more money you make, the greater your potential to enhance and enrich the lives of others. By creating jobs, improving services, and investing in societal progress, you not only build personal wealth but also contribute to the well-being and advancement of those around you. Embracing the idea that wealth enables you to offer more value and make a positive difference helps transform the narrative around financial success into one of empowerment and opportunity.

Identifying Your Money Mindset

One of the first steps in unpacking your money story is to identify these underlying messages and beliefs. Start by reflecting on the money-related messages you received growing up. Were there specific phrases or attitudes about money that you remember vividly? Write them down. Next, think about how these beliefs have influenced your financial behavior. For instance, if you were taught that debt is always bad, you might avoid taking on any form of credit, even when it could be strategically beneficial.

Another crucial aspect of understanding your money story is recognizing how your financial beliefs might be limiting your potential. Do you hold beliefs that are preventing you from taking financial risks or pursuing opportunities? For example, if you believe that investing is only for the wealthy, you might hesitate to invest even small amounts of money, missing out on growth opportunities.

Let's not forget the role of societal and cultural expectations. Perhaps you feel pressured to live up to a certain standard of success or wealth that doesn't align with your personal values or goals. These external pressures can create internal conflict and hinder your ability to make financial decisions that are right for you.

To begin rewriting your money story, start by questioning these ingrained beliefs. Ask yourself if they are based on your own experiences or simply adopted from others. Are they serving your financial goals, or are they holding you back? Challenge these beliefs by seeking out new information and perspectives. Surround yourself with people who have a positive and proactive approach to money, and educate yourself on financial topics that can help reshape your understanding.

By unpacking your money story and identifying the messages and beliefs that have shaped it, you can begin the process of transformation. This self-awareness is crucial for rewriting your narrative and creating a money story that supports your financial success. In the next section, we'll explore how to actively rewrite these narratives and replace them with empowering beliefs that will set you on the path to financial abundance.

Understanding and identifying your current money mindset is the foundational step towards financial transformation. Your mindset influences every financial decision you make, from budgeting and investing to spending and saving. So now let's explore how to assess your existing beliefs about money, whether they are rooted in scarcity, fear, or abundance, and provide practical exercises to guide you through this self-discovery process.

To begin identifying your current money mindset, start with these exercises:

1. **Reflective Journaling**: Take time to reflect on your beliefs about money by journaling. Write down your thoughts on the following prompts: "What are my earliest memories of money?" "How do I feel about wealth and success?" "What are my biggest financial fears?" and "What does financial security mean to me?" Your responses will reveal underlying beliefs and attitudes about money.
2. **Money Beliefs Assessment**: Create a list of statements related to money and rate your agreement with each on a scale from 1 to 5, where 1 is strongly disagree and 5 is strongly agree. Examples of statements include: "Money is the root of all evil," "There is never enough

money," "I am capable of achieving financial success," and "Wealth is accessible to everyone." Analyze your ratings to identify whether your beliefs lean towards scarcity, fear, or abundance.

3. **Financial Behavior Analysis**: Examine your financial behaviors and patterns. Are you frequently anxious about money, or do you tend to avoid financial planning altogether? Do you make impulsive purchases or struggle with saving? Your financial behaviors can offer insights into your mindset. For example, if you find yourself avoiding investments due to fear of loss, this may indicate a scarcity mindset.

In summary, identifying your current money mindset involves introspection and practical exercises that reveal your underlying beliefs and attitudes about money. By examining your reflections, money beliefs, and financial behaviors, you can gain insight into whether your mindset is rooted in scarcity, fear, or abundance. And then afterwards, you can start to redefine your relationship to money.

Start by Challenging Negative Beliefs

Begin by questioning the validity of your existing money beliefs. Ask yourself: Are these beliefs based on actual experiences, or are they just echoes of past messages? For instance, if you've always believed that "money is the root of all evil," consider where this belief originated and whether it holds true in your life. Often, negative beliefs about money are generalized and not reflective of reality.

Take the belief that "I'm not good with money." This is a common narrative for many, often based on past mistakes or lack of financial education. To challenge this belief, consider the steps you've taken to improve your financial literacy. Have you read books, attended workshops, or sought advice from financial experts? Recognize your efforts and progress, and remind yourself that financial skills can be developed with practice and knowledge.

Replace Negative Beliefs with Empowering Narratives

Once you've identified and challenged negative beliefs, it's time to replace them with positive, empowering narratives. This involves actively creating and adopting new beliefs that align with your financial goals and aspirations.

For instance, if you previously believed that "wealth is reserved for the lucky few," replace it with a belief like "financial success is achievable through smart choices and perseverance." Write down these new beliefs and make them a daily affirmation. Repeat them regularly to reinforce this positive mindset.

Create a vision board that reflects your new money story. Include images and words that represent your financial goals, such as owning a home, starting a business, or achieving financial independence. This visual representation serves as a constant reminder of the success you're working towards and helps solidify your new beliefs.

Visualize Your New Money Story

Visualization is a powerful tool for reshaping your money story. Take a few minutes each day to imagine yourself living out your new financial narrative. Picture yourself confidently managing your finances, making successful investments, and achieving your financial goals. This practice not only helps reinforce your new beliefs but also creates a sense of excitement and motivation.

Dream boards and vision boards are powerful tools for manifesting your goals and shaping your financial future. These visual representations of your aspirations serve as daily reminders of what you're striving for, helping to keep your dreams front and center. To make them truly effective, it's crucial to engage with them emotionally—feel the abundance and gratitude for the achievements and possessions you desire, even if you don't yet have them. By regularly visualizing these goals and immersing yourself in the emotions associated with achieving them, you create a magnetic force that attracts opportunities and reprograms your subconscious mind to align with the mindset of a successful, wealthy individual. Constantly viewing your vision board not only keeps your objectives in focus but also reinforces a positive and abundant mindset, making it easier to recognize and seize opportunities as they arise.

This ongoing emotional connection helps solidify your belief in your ability to achieve your goals and transforms your financial reality.

In my own journey, visualization played a crucial role. I vividly imagined the success of my real estate ventures and the growth of my investment portfolio. This mental rehearsal helped me approach opportunities with confidence and enthusiasm, leading to tangible results. Seeing my dream board from years ago become a reality has been an unreal experience that I want everyone to experience in their lives.

Surround Yourself with Positive Influences

The people you associate with and the content you consume can significantly impact your money mindset. Seek out mentors, peers, and communities that share your positive financial outlook and can offer support and encouragement. Engage with books, podcasts, and blogs that promote financial literacy and success.

For instance, connecting with a financial mentor who embodies the mindset and success you aspire to can provide invaluable guidance and inspiration. Join online forums or local groups focused on financial empowerment, where you can exchange ideas and learn from others who are also working on transforming their money stories.

Practice Gratitude and Self-Compassion

Gratitude and self-compassion are essential in the process of rewriting your money story. Regularly acknowledge and appreciate the progress you've made, no matter how small. Keep a gratitude journal where you write down things you're thankful for in relation to your finances. This is a side note, but practicing gratitude is also an amazing cure for anxiety and depression that I can personally attest to.

Self-compassion is equally important. Understand that changing deeply ingrained beliefs takes time and effort. Be patient with yourself and celebrate your successes along the way. Recognize that setbacks are part of the journey and use them as opportunities for growth!

Embrace the Process of Transformation

Embracing change is essential on your journey to financial growth. As you start to transform your mindset and habits around money, you'll notice that your entire world begins to shift. Your friendships, environment, and even your daily routines will evolve, often in ways you never imagined. This growth is necessary and should be welcomed, not resisted. You'll find yourself surrounded by people who uplift and inspire you, in environments that foster your success. The key is to stay open to this transformation, understanding that it's all part of the process. You're not just changing your bank account—you're evolving into a more empowered, successful version of yourself. So, lean into the change, knowing that it's paving the way for a brighter, more abundant future. Embrace this process with confidence, and remember that every step you take toward a new financial narrative brings you closer to achieving the success you deserve.

Chapter 3: Building a Solid Financial Foundation

Once you start changing your subconscious beliefs surrounding money and wealth, you are now ready to work on becoming more financially literate. First off, to achieve lasting financial success, you need to establish a solid financial foundation. This is the bedrock upon which all future wealth-building efforts are built. Without a strong foundation, even the most ambitious financial goals can crumble under the weight of poor planning or mismanagement. Chapter 3 will be about exploring the essential components of a solid financial foundation, including budgeting, saving, and managing debt.

Creating a Budget

The cornerstone of financial stability is a well-constructed budget. A budget is more than just a list of your income and expenses; it's a strategic tool that helps you track your spending, plan for the future, and ensure that you're living within your means. Start by recording all sources of income, including your salary, any side hustles, and investment returns. Then, list all your expenses, from fixed costs like rent and utilities to variable costs like dining out and entertainment.

Once you have a comprehensive view of your income and expenses, categorize your spending to identify areas where you might be overspending. Are you allocating too much to discretionary items, such as shopping or dining out, at the expense of your savings? By pinpointing these areas, you can make informed decisions about where to cut back and how to reallocate funds toward more productive uses.

For effective budgeting, consider using the 50/30/20 rule: allocate 50% of your income to necessities (like housing and groceries), 30% to discretionary spending (such as entertainment and hobbies), and 20% to savings and debt repayment. This rule provides a balanced approach that ensures you're covering your needs, enjoying your life, and building a financial cushion.

Building an Emergency Fund

An emergency fund is a crucial element of your financial foundation. This fund acts as a financial safety net, protecting you from unexpected expenses like medical emergencies, car repairs, or job loss. Financial experts typically recommend saving three to six months' worth of living expenses in an easily accessible account. By having an emergency fund, you can avoid falling into debt when life gives you unexpected financial setbacks and you can rest easy knowing you have a backup plan.

To build your emergency fund, start by setting a small, achievable goal—say, $500 or $1,000. Once you reach this initial target, gradually increase your savings until you have the full amount needed. Automate your savings by setting up a direct deposit from your paycheck into your emergency fund. This ensures that you consistently contribute to your fund without having to think about it.

Managing and Reducing Debt

Effective debt management is another critical aspect of building a solid financial foundation. High-interest debt, such as credit card balances, can quickly spiral out of control and hinder your financial progress. To tackle debt, begin by listing all your debts, including the amount owed, interest rates, and minimum payments.

One popular method for debt repayment is the snowball method. Start by paying off your smallest debt first while making minimum payments on larger debts. Once the smallest debt is paid off, apply the amount you were paying on that debt to the next smallest debt. This approach creates momentum and motivates you as you see your debts being eliminated one by one.

Alternatively, you might consider the avalanche method, where you focus on paying off debts with the highest interest rates first. This strategy saves you more money in interest over time but may require more patience, as the progress might be slower initially.

Tracking Your Progress

Regularly reviewing and adjusting your financial plan is essential for maintaining a solid foundation. Track your spending, monitor your savings progress, and reassess your budget as needed. Life changes, such as a new job, a move, or a significant purchase, can impact your financial situation, and your plan should adapt accordingly.

In summary, building a solid financial foundation involves creating a budget, establishing an emergency fund, managing debt, and continuously tracking your progress. These steps not only provide stability but also set the stage for more advanced financial strategies and wealth-building opportunities. By laying this groundwork, you'll be well-prepared to tackle more ambitious financial goals and achieve long-term success.

Now that we've covered the essentials of budgeting, saving, and debt management, let's delve into additional strategies that will fortify your financial foundation and set the stage for future growth.

Investing in Your Future

Once you have a solid budget, emergency fund, and a plan to manage debt, it's time to think about investing. Investing is crucial for building wealth over time and achieving long-term financial goals. Start by educating yourself about different investment options, such as stocks, bonds, mutual funds, and real estate. Each type of investment carries its own risk and potential return, so it's important to choose investments that align with your risk tolerance and financial objectives.

A good starting point for beginners is to invest in low-cost index funds or exchange-traded funds (ETFs). These funds offer diversification by pooling your money into a broad range of assets, which can help mitigate risk and provide steady returns over time. Consider setting up a retirement account, such as a 401(k) or IRA, to take advantage of tax benefits and compound growth. Automate your investments by setting up regular contributions from your paycheck or bank account. This approach, known as dollar-cost averaging, helps you invest consistently and avoid the pitfalls of market timing.

Setting Financial Goals

Setting clear financial goals is a key component of a robust financial foundation. Goals provide direction and motivation, helping you stay focused on what you want to achieve. Start by defining both short-term and long-term goals. Short-term goals might include saving for a vacation, paying off a small debt, or building a new emergency fund. Long-term goals could involve saving for a home, funding your children's education, or planning for retirement.

Create SMART goals—Specific, Measurable, Achievable, Relevant, and Time-bound. For example, instead of setting a vague goal like "I want to save more money," specify "I will save $5,000 for a down payment on a car within the next 12 months." Breaking down larger goals into smaller, manageable steps makes them less overwhelming and easier to track.

Building a Strong Credit Score

A strong credit score is an essential part of a solid financial foundation. Your credit score affects your ability to secure loans, obtain favorable interest rates, and even influence your insurance premiums. To build and maintain a strong credit score, focus on the following practices:

1. **Pay Your Bills On Time:** Timely payment of bills, including credit cards, loans, and utilities, is crucial for maintaining a good credit score. Set up automatic payments or reminders to ensure you never miss a due date.
2. **Keep Credit Utilization Low:** Aim to use less than 30% of your available credit on credit cards. High credit utilization can negatively impact your credit score.
3. **Monitor Your Credit Report:** Regularly review your credit report for errors or inaccuracies. You can obtain a free copy of your credit report from major credit bureaus once a year. Dispute any errors promptly to ensure your credit report reflects accurate information.
4. **Maintain a Healthy Credit Mix:** Having a diverse credit mix, including credit cards, installment loans, and retail accounts, can positively impact your credit score.

However, only open credit accounts that you need and can manage responsibly.

Protecting Your Financial Foundation

Protecting your financial foundation involves safeguarding your assets and planning for unexpected events. Consider purchasing insurance coverage, such as health, auto, home, and life insurance, to protect yourself and your family from financial setbacks. Additionally, create a will and establish an estate plan to ensure your assets are distributed according to your wishes in the event of your passing.

Building a solid financial foundation is an ongoing process that requires dedication and regular review. By establishing a budget, saving diligently, managing debt effectively, investing wisely, setting clear goals, maintaining a strong credit score, and protecting your assets, you'll lay the groundwork for long-term financial success. This foundation not only provides stability but also positions you to take advantage of future opportunities and achieve your financial dreams.

Chapter 4: Mastering the Art of Smart Investing

In this chapter, we'll explore the fundamentals of smart investing—a critical component for building and sustaining wealth. Investing wisely involves understanding various asset classes, developing a strategic approach, and continuously educating yourself about market trends. Whether you're just starting out or looking to refine your investment strategy, mastering these principles will set you on the path to financial growth and stability.

Understanding Different Asset Classes

The first step in smart investing is to familiarize yourself with different asset classes and their unique characteristics. The most common asset classes include stocks, bonds, real estate, and cash equivalents. Each has its own risk profile, return potential, and role in a diversified investment portfolio.

1. **Stocks:** Stocks represent ownership in a company and offer the potential for high returns through capital appreciation and dividends. However, they also come with higher volatility and risk. When investing in stocks, consider diversifying across different sectors and industries to mitigate risk. Research companies thoroughly and understand their financial health, competitive position, and growth prospects.

2. **Bonds**: Bonds are fixed-income securities that provide regular interest payments and return the principal amount at maturity. They are generally less volatile than stocks and can provide steady income. Bonds come in various forms, including government bonds, corporate bonds, and municipal bonds. Assess the credit quality and interest rate environment before investing in bonds, as these factors can impact bond performance.
3. **Real Estate**: Real estate investing involves purchasing properties for rental income or capital appreciation. Real estate can offer steady cash flow and potential tax benefits, but it also requires significant capital and management. Evaluate the local real estate market, property condition, and potential rental income before investing. Consider different real estate strategies, such as residential, commercial, or REITs (Real Estate Investment Trusts), based on your investment goals.
4. **Cash Equivalents**: Cash equivalents, such as savings accounts, money market funds, and certificates of deposit (CDs), offer low-risk, low-return investments. They are ideal for short-term goals or emergency funds due to their liquidity and stability. While they provide safety, they typically offer lower returns compared to other asset classes.

Developing an Investment Strategy

Once you understand the different asset classes, it's important to develop a well-defined investment strategy that aligns with your financial goals, risk tolerance, and time horizon. A solid investment strategy involves asset allocation, diversification, and periodic rebalancing.

1. **Asset Allocation:** Asset allocation is the process of dividing your investment portfolio among different asset classes based on your risk tolerance and investment objectives. A balanced portfolio might include a mix of stocks, bonds, and real estate to achieve a desirable level of risk and return. For instance, younger investors with a longer time horizon may allocate a larger portion to stocks for growth, while those nearing retirement might shift towards bonds for stability.

2. **Diversification:** Diversification involves spreading your investments across various assets, sectors, and geographic regions to reduce risk. By diversifying, you minimize the impact of poor performance in any single investment on your overall portfolio. For example, investing in a variety of stocks across different industries and geographic locations helps mitigate the risk associated with economic downturns in a specific sector or region.

3. **Periodic Rebalancing:** Over time, the performance of different asset classes can cause your portfolio to drift away from its intended allocation. Periodic rebalancing involves reviewing and adjusting your portfolio to maintain your desired asset allocation. This ensures that you're not overly exposed to any single asset class and helps manage risk effectively.

Setting Clear Investment Goals

Establishing clear investment goals is essential for developing a successful investment strategy. Define your short-term and long-term goals, such as saving for a down payment on a house, funding your child's education, or planning for retirement. Each goal may require a different investment approach, so tailor your strategy accordingly. Consider factors such as the time horizon, required return, and risk tolerance for each goal. For example, short-term goals might be best served by lower-risk investments, while long-term goals can benefit from higher-risk, higher-return investments.

In summary, mastering smart investing involves understanding different asset classes, developing a strategic approach, and setting clear investment goals. By familiarizing yourself with various investments, creating a well-diversified portfolio, and regularly reviewing your strategy, you'll be well-positioned to achieve financial growth and stability. In the next section, we'll delve deeper into advanced investment strategies and techniques to further enhance your investment acumen and success.

With a foundational understanding of different asset classes and a strategic approach to investing, it's time to delve into more advanced investment strategies and techniques that can further enhance your financial success. These strategies involve understanding market trends, leveraging tax advantages, and utilizing sophisticated investment vehicles.

Market Trends and Economic Indicators

Successful investing requires staying informed about market trends and economic indicators that can impact your investments. Economic indicators such as inflation rates, interest rates, and employment data provide insights into the health of the economy and can influence investment decisions.

1. **Economic Indicators:** Inflation, interest rates, and GDP growth are critical indicators that affect various asset classes. For example, rising inflation can erode the purchasing power of fixed-income investments like bonds, while interest rate changes can impact stock valuations. Understanding these indicators helps you make informed decisions about when to buy or sell assets and how to adjust your portfolio based on prevailing economic conditions.
2. **Market Trends:** Keeping an eye on market trends and sector performance can provide valuable information for making investment decisions. For instance, technological advancements or shifts in consumer behavior can create growth opportunities in specific sectors, such as technology or renewable energy. Stay updated with financial news, market reports, and industry analyses to identify emerging trends and adjust your investments accordingly.

Leveraging Tax Advantages

Investing with tax efficiency in mind can significantly enhance your overall returns. Various investment accounts and strategies offer tax advantages that can help you keep more of your earnings. Here are some key tax-efficient strategies:

1. **Tax-Advantaged Accounts**: Utilize accounts like 401(k)s, IRAs, and Roth IRAs, which offer tax benefits for retirement savings. Contributions to a traditional 401(k) or IRA are typically tax-deductible, reducing your taxable income in the year you contribute. Roth IRAs, on the other hand, allow for tax-free withdrawals in retirement, provided certain conditions are met.
2. **Capital Gains Management**: Capital gains are profits earned from selling investments at a higher price than their purchase price. Long-term capital gains (from assets held for more than a year) are usually taxed at a lower rate than short-term gains. By holding investments for the long term, you can benefit from these lower tax rates. Additionally, consider tax-loss harvesting—selling investments that have declined in value to offset gains and reduce your overall tax liability.
3. **Dividend Income**: Dividends received from investments are often taxed at a different rate than regular income. Qualified dividends, typically paid by U.S. corporations and held for a certain period, are taxed at a lower rate. Understanding the tax treatment of dividend

income can help you optimize your investment strategy for tax efficiency.

Utilizing Advanced Investment Vehicles

For more sophisticated investors, exploring advanced investment vehicles can offer additional opportunities for growth and diversification. Here are a few examples:

1. **Exchange-Traded Funds (ETFs)**: ETFs are investment funds that trade on stock exchanges and offer diversification across various assets or sectors. Unlike mutual funds, ETFs can be bought and sold throughout the trading day, providing flexibility and liquidity. Some ETFs focus on specific strategies, such as dividend growth or sector rotation, allowing you to tailor your investments to your goals.

2. **Real Estate Investment Trusts (REITs)**: REITs are companies that own, operate, or finance income-producing real estate. Investing in REITs allows you to gain exposure to real estate markets without directly owning property. REITs often provide attractive dividend yields and can be an effective way to diversify your portfolio with real estate exposure.

3. **Alternative Investments**: Consider exploring alternative investments such as private equity, hedge funds, or commodities. These investments can offer unique growth opportunities and diversification but often come with higher risks and may require a higher minimum

investment. Assess your risk tolerance and investment objectives before venturing into alternatives.

Regular Portfolio Review and Adjustment

Maintaining a successful investment strategy requires regular portfolio review and adjustment. Periodically evaluate your investment performance, re-assess your goals, and make necessary adjustments to stay on track. Market conditions, personal circumstances, and financial goals can change over time, and your investment strategy should evolve accordingly.

In summary, mastering smart investing involves understanding market trends, leveraging tax advantages, and exploring advanced investment vehicles. By staying informed, utilizing tax-efficient strategies, and regularly reviewing your portfolio, you can optimize your investments and work towards achieving your financial goals.

Chapter 5: Scaling Your Investments and Creating Multiple Streams of Income

With a solid investment foundation in place, the next step is to scale your investments and explore strategies for creating multiple streams of income. Diversification and income diversification are key to enhancing your financial stability and growth. This chapter will cover advanced strategies for scaling your investments and the importance of developing various income streams to build long-term wealth.

Scaling Your Investments

Scaling your investments involves increasing the size of your investment portfolio and expanding into new asset classes or strategies to grow your wealth. This process requires a careful balance of risk management and strategic planning. Here are some strategies to consider for scaling your investments:

1. **Reinvesting Returns**: One of the simplest ways to scale your investments is by reinvesting the returns you earn. Whether through dividends, interest, or capital gains, reinvesting these earnings into additional investments allows your portfolio to grow exponentially over time. For instance, if you receive dividends from stocks or mutual funds, use these dividends to purchase more shares, thereby compounding your investment returns.

2. **Increasing Contributions**: Gradually increasing your investment contributions is another effective way to scale your investments. As your income grows or your financial situation improves, allocate a higher percentage of your earnings toward investments. Consistent, incremental increases in contributions can significantly boost your portfolio's growth over the long term.
3. **Exploring New Asset Classes**: Diversifying into new asset classes can provide additional growth opportunities and spread risk. For example, if you have primarily invested in stocks and bonds, consider adding real estate, commodities, or alternative investments to your portfolio. Each asset class has unique characteristics and can respond differently to market conditions, enhancing your portfolio's overall resilience.
4. **Leveraging Investment Accounts**: Utilize various investment accounts to optimize growth and tax efficiency. For instance, contributing to tax-advantaged accounts like Roth IRAs or 401(k)s can offer long-term growth potential and tax benefits. Additionally, consider using taxable brokerage accounts for investments that don't fit within retirement account limits or for short-term goals.

Creating Multiple Streams of Income

Diversifying your income sources is crucial for financial stability and growth. Multiple streams of income can provide a buffer against economic uncertainties and create opportunities for wealth accumulation. Here are several strategies for generating additional income:

1. **Side Hustles and Freelancing**: Leveraging your skills and expertise through side hustles or freelance work can provide a significant boost to your income. Whether it's consulting, writing, graphic design, or tutoring, side gigs offer flexibility and the potential to earn extra money outside of your primary job. Identify opportunities that align with your skills and interests to maximize your earning potential.

2. **Real Estate Investments**: Investing in rental properties or real estate can generate a steady stream of passive income. Rental properties provide regular income through lease payments and potential appreciation in property value. When investing in real estate, consider factors such as location, property management, and market trends to ensure a successful investment.

3. **Dividend Stocks**: Dividend-paying stocks offer a regular income stream in addition to potential capital gains. Invest in companies with a history of consistent dividend payments and a strong track record of financial stability. Dividends can be reinvested or used as a source of income, depending on your financial goals.

4. **Peer-to-Peer Lending**: Peer-to-peer (P2P) lending platforms connect borrowers with individual lenders, allowing you to earn interest on your loans. By investing in P2P lending, you can diversify your income sources and potentially earn higher returns compared to traditional

savings accounts. However, be aware of the risks involved, including borrower defaults, and diversify your investments across multiple loans to mitigate risk.

5. **Creating Digital Products:** Develop and sell digital products, such as eBooks, online courses, or software, to generate passive income. Once created, digital products can be sold repeatedly with minimal ongoing effort. Focus on creating high-quality content that addresses specific needs or interests within your target market.

Scaling and Diversifying Investments

Scaling your investments and creating multiple income streams go hand in hand. As your financial situation improves, reinvest your returns, increase contributions, and explore new asset classes. Simultaneously, develop and manage diverse income sources to build a robust financial foundation. By integrating these strategies, you can enhance your wealth-building efforts and achieve long-term financial success.

In the next section, we'll explore advanced strategies for managing risk and optimizing returns, ensuring that your scaled investments and multiple income streams are effectively aligned with your financial goals.

As we delve deeper into scaling your investments and creating multiple income streams, it's important to address strategies for managing risk, optimizing returns, and ensuring your diverse income sources are working harmoniously. These advanced techniques will help you maximize the effectiveness of your financial strategies and safeguard your wealth.

Managing Risk Effectively

While scaling your investments and diversifying income sources can enhance financial stability, managing risk remains crucial. Effective risk management helps protect your portfolio from significant losses and ensures long-term success. Here are key strategies for managing risk:

1. **Diversification:** Diversification is one of the most effective ways to manage investment risk. By spreading your investments across various asset classes, sectors, and geographic regions, you reduce the impact of poor performance in any single area. A well-diversified portfolio can help buffer against market volatility and improve overall returns.
2. **Risk Tolerance Assessment:** Regularly assess your risk tolerance to ensure your investment strategy aligns with your comfort level and financial goals. Risk tolerance is influenced by factors such as age, income, financial goals, and investment horizon. As you approach significant life events or near retirement, you may need to adjust your portfolio to reduce exposure to high-risk assets and focus on more stable investments.

3. **Asset Allocation Rebalancing**: Periodically review and rebalance your asset allocation to maintain your desired risk level. Over time, the performance of different investments can cause your portfolio to deviate from its original allocation. Rebalancing involves adjusting your holdings to realign with your target asset allocation, helping to manage risk and optimize returns.
4. **Hedging Strategies**: Hedging involves using financial instruments or strategies to offset potential losses in your investments. For example, options and futures contracts can be used to hedge against market downturns or fluctuations in specific asset prices. While hedging can help mitigate risk, it can also involve additional costs and complexities. Evaluate whether hedging aligns with your investment strategy and risk tolerance.

Optimizing Returns

Maximizing returns is essential for building wealth and achieving financial goals. To optimize returns, consider the following strategies:

1. **Active vs. Passive Investing**: Decide between active and passive investing strategies based on your investment philosophy and goals. Active investing involves selecting individual stocks or assets with the aim of outperforming the market, while passive investing focuses on tracking market indices through index funds or ETFs. Each approach has its advantages and potential risks, so choose

the one that aligns with your preferences and investment strategy.

2. **Tax-Efficient Investing:** Implement tax-efficient strategies to enhance your returns by minimizing tax liabilities. For example, invest in tax-advantaged accounts like Roth IRAs or 401(k)s to benefit from tax-free growth or deductions. Additionally, consider tax-loss harvesting to offset capital gains with losses and manage taxable income.

3. **Dividend Reinvestment:** Reinvest dividends earned from dividend-paying stocks or funds to compound your investment returns. Dividend reinvestment plans (DRIPs) automatically purchase additional shares with the dividends received, allowing you to benefit from compound growth and increase your investment holdings over time.

Ensuring Income Streams Work Harmoniously

For a successful financial strategy, ensure your multiple income streams work together effectively:

1. **Income Integration:** Integrate various income sources into a cohesive financial plan. For example, combine income from side hustles, real estate investments, and dividends with your primary earnings to create a comprehensive budget and investment strategy. Ensure that each income stream complements your overall financial goals and provides a balanced approach to wealth building.

2. **Monitor and Adjust:** Regularly monitor the performance of your income sources and make adjustments

as needed. Assess the profitability of side hustles, track rental income, and review the performance of dividend stocks. Adjust your strategies based on changes in income, market conditions, or personal goals to maintain financial stability and growth.

3. **Emergency Preparedness:** Prepare for potential disruptions to your income streams by maintaining an emergency fund and having contingency plans. An emergency fund can provide a financial cushion in case of unexpected events, such as job loss or economic downturns, helping you maintain stability and continue investing effectively.

In conclusion, scaling your investments and creating multiple income streams involves careful risk management, strategic optimization, and ensuring that all components of your financial plan work together harmoniously. By diversifying your investments, optimizing returns, and integrating income sources, you can build a robust financial foundation that supports long-term wealth and success. In the next chapter, we'll explore advanced financial planning techniques and strategies for achieving your most ambitious financial goals.

Chapter 6: Advanced Financial Planning Techniques

So now it is time to talk about advanced financial planning techniques that go beyond the basics of budgeting and investing. These strategies will help you fine-tune your financial approach, optimize your wealth management, and achieve your most ambitious financial goals. We'll explore estate planning, tax strategies, and retirement planning to ensure your financial strategy is comprehensive and effective.

Estate Planning: Securing Your Legacy

Estate planning is crucial for managing how your assets will be distributed after your passing. Effective estate planning not only ensures that your wishes are honored but also helps minimize potential taxes and legal complexities for your heirs. Here are key components of a robust estate plan:

1. **Creating a Will:** A will is a legal document that specifies how your assets should be distributed after your death. It allows you to designate beneficiaries, appoint an executor to manage your estate, and provide instructions for any dependents. Regularly update your will to reflect changes in your life, such as marriage, divorce, or the birth of children.

2. **Establishing a Trust:** Trusts can offer additional benefits, such as avoiding probate, reducing estate taxes, and providing more control over asset distribution. There are various types of trusts, including revocable living trusts and irrevocable trusts. A revocable living trust allows you to retain control over the assets during your lifetime and can be modified or revoked as needed. An irrevocable trust, on the other hand, typically offers more significant tax benefits but requires relinquishing control over the assets.
3. **Power of Attorney and Healthcare Directives:** Designate a power of attorney to make financial decisions on your behalf if you become incapacitated. Additionally, establish healthcare directives or a living will to outline your medical preferences and appoint someone to make healthcare decisions for you. These documents ensure that your wishes are followed and provide clarity for your family during challenging times.
4. **Beneficiary Designations:** Review and update beneficiary designations on accounts such as life insurance policies, retirement accounts, and investment accounts. Beneficiary designations override instructions in your will or trust, so it's essential to keep them current to ensure your assets are distributed according to your wishes.

Tax Strategies: Maximizing Efficiency

Implementing tax strategies can help you minimize tax liabilities and maximize your investment returns. Effective tax planning involves understanding how different investments and financial decisions impact your taxes. Here are some strategies to consider:

1. **Tax-Advantaged Accounts**: Utilize tax-advantaged accounts to benefit from tax breaks and defer taxes. Contributing to retirement accounts like 401(k)s or IRAs allows you to reduce your taxable income while saving for retirement. Roth IRAs offer tax-free growth and withdrawals in retirement. Additionally, consider health savings accounts (HSAs) for tax-free medical expense savings.

2. **Tax-Efficient Investment Strategies**: Focus on tax-efficient investing to minimize your tax liabilities. Invest in assets that generate favorable tax treatment, such as qualified dividend stocks and long-term capital gains. Avoid frequent trading and short-term capital gains, which can lead to higher tax rates. Tax-loss harvesting, where you sell investments at a loss to offset gains, can also help reduce your taxable income.

3. **Income Splitting**: Explore income splitting strategies to reduce your overall tax burden. Income splitting involves distributing income among family members in lower tax brackets to lower the total tax liability. For example, you can gift assets to family members or utilize family trusts to allocate income more efficiently. Be aware of gift tax limits and consult with a tax advisor to ensure compliance with tax regulations.

4. **Charitable Contributions**: Consider making charitable contributions to benefit from tax deductions.

Donating appreciated assets, such as stocks or real estate, can provide tax advantages while supporting causes you care about. Donor-advised funds offer a way to manage charitable donations and potentially receive immediate tax benefits.

Retirement Planning: Preparing for the Future

Effective retirement planning is essential for ensuring that you have sufficient resources to maintain your desired lifestyle in retirement. Here are key elements of a comprehensive retirement plan:

1. **Calculating Retirement Needs**: Estimate your retirement needs based on factors such as desired lifestyle, expected expenses, and longevity. Use retirement calculators and financial planning tools to determine how much you need to save and invest to achieve your retirement goals. Consider factors like inflation, healthcare costs, and potential changes in income sources.

2. **Developing a Retirement Savings Strategy**: Create a strategy for saving and investing for retirement. Contribute regularly to retirement accounts, such as 401(k)s, IRAs, or Roth IRAs. Take advantage of employer matching contributions and increase your savings rate as your income grows. Diversify your investments to balance growth potential and risk.

3. **Planning for Withdrawals**: Develop a strategy for withdrawing funds from your retirement accounts.

Consider factors such as tax implications, required minimum distributions (RMDs), and your overall withdrawal strategy. Aim to create a sustainable withdrawal plan that ensures your funds last throughout retirement.

In summary, advanced financial planning techniques—such as estate planning, tax strategies, and retirement planning—are essential for optimizing your wealth management and achieving long-term financial goals. By implementing these strategies, you can secure your legacy, minimize tax liabilities, and prepare effectively for retirement.

As we continue exploring advanced financial planning techniques, we'll focus on navigating financial challenges, making strategic decisions, and optimizing your financial strategy to adapt to changing circumstances. This part of the chapter will provide insights into overcoming obstacles and making informed decisions to ensure sustained wealth and financial success.

Navigating Financial Challenges

Financial challenges are inevitable, and having a strategy to address them is crucial for maintaining financial stability and growth. Here are key approaches to effectively navigate these challenges:

1. **Emergency Funds**: Building and maintaining an emergency fund is fundamental for managing unexpected

financial setbacks, such as job loss, medical emergencies, or major repairs. Aim to save three to six months' worth of living expenses in a liquid, easily accessible account. An emergency fund provides a financial cushion and helps you avoid dipping into long-term investments or incurring debt during challenging times.

2. **Debt Management:** Managing debt effectively is essential for financial health. Prioritize paying down high-interest debt, such as credit card balances, to reduce interest costs and free up resources for investing and saving. Consider strategies like the debt snowball or debt avalanche methods to systematically tackle debt. If necessary, explore consolidation options or work with a financial advisor to create a manageable debt repayment plan.

3. **Insurance Planning:** Adequate insurance coverage protects against financial risks and provides peace of mind. Review your insurance needs regularly to ensure you have appropriate coverage for health, life, disability, property, and liability. Evaluate policy terms, coverage limits, and deductibles to ensure you're adequately protected and avoid potential gaps in coverage.

4. **Contingency Planning:** Develop contingency plans for potential financial disruptions, such as job loss or economic downturns. This may include diversifying income sources, reducing discretionary spending, or adjusting investment strategies. Regularly review and

update your contingency plans to ensure they align with your current financial situation and goals.

Making Strategic Financial Decisions

Strategic decision-making is crucial for optimizing your financial strategy and achieving long-term success. Here are key considerations for making informed financial decisions:

1. **Evaluating Investment Opportunities**: When considering new investment opportunities, conduct thorough research and due diligence. Assess factors such as potential returns, risks, market conditions, and alignment with your financial goals. Seek advice from financial professionals and consider the impact on your overall portfolio before committing to new investments.
2. **Timing Major Financial Moves**: Timing can significantly impact the success of major financial decisions, such as buying a home, starting a business, or making large investments. Evaluate market conditions, economic indicators, and personal circumstances to determine the optimal timing for these decisions. Avoid making impulsive decisions based on short-term market fluctuations or emotional responses.
3. **Seeking Professional Advice**: Consulting with financial advisors, tax professionals, or estate planners can provide valuable insights and guidance. Professionals can help you navigate complex financial situations, optimize

your strategies, and ensure compliance with regulations. Choose advisors with relevant expertise and a fiduciary responsibility to act in your best interest.

4. **Regular Financial Reviews**: Conduct regular reviews of your financial plan to ensure it remains aligned with your goals and circumstances. Review your investment performance, budget, and financial objectives periodically to identify any necessary adjustments. Regular reviews help you stay on track and make informed decisions based on current information.

Adapting to Changing Circumstances

Financial planning is an ongoing process that requires adaptability to changing circumstances. Here's how to effectively adapt your financial strategy:

1. **Adjusting Goals and Strategies**: Life events, such as career changes, family growth, or economic shifts, can impact your financial goals and strategies. Be prepared to adjust your goals and strategies based on these changes. For example, if you receive a promotion or bonus, consider reallocating funds toward increased savings or investments.

2. **Embracing New Opportunities**: Stay open to new financial opportunities and trends that align with your goals. This may include exploring innovative investment options, taking advantage of emerging technologies, or pursuing additional income streams. Staying informed and

adaptable can help you capitalize on opportunities for growth and success.

3. **Managing Risks and Uncertainties:** Financial markets and economic conditions are inherently uncertain. Develop a flexible financial plan that accounts for potential risks and uncertainties. Use risk management strategies, such as diversification and insurance, to protect your assets and adapt to changing conditions.

In summary, advanced financial planning involves navigating financial challenges, making strategic decisions, and adapting to changing circumstances. By implementing effective risk management, optimizing your financial strategies, and staying adaptable, you can enhance your financial stability and achieve long-term success. In the next chapter, we'll explore how to leverage financial technology and tools to further enhance your financial planning and investment strategies.

Chapter 7: Leveraging Financial Technology and Tools

In today's rapidly evolving financial landscape, leveraging financial technology (fintech) and tools can provide a significant edge in managing your finances, optimizing investments, and achieving your financial goals. This chapter will explore how to effectively use financial technology to enhance your financial planning, streamline processes, and make informed decisions.

Embracing Fintech Innovations

Financial technology has revolutionized the way we manage and grow our finances. From budgeting apps to investment platforms, fintech innovations offer a range of tools designed to simplify and enhance financial management. Here's how to embrace these innovations:

1. **Budgeting and Expense Tracking Apps**: Modern budgeting apps, such as Mint, YNAB (You Need a Budget), and PocketGuard, provide powerful features for tracking expenses, setting budgets, and managing your finances. These apps connect to your bank accounts and credit cards, automatically categorizing transactions and offering insights into your spending habits. By using these tools, you can easily monitor your budget, identify areas for improvement, and stay on top of your financial goals.

2. **Automated Savings Tools:** Automated savings tools, like Digit and Acorns, help you save effortlessly by automatically transferring small amounts of money into savings or investment accounts. Digit analyzes your spending patterns and transfers surplus funds to your savings account, while Acorns rounds up your purchases and invests the spare change. These tools make saving and investing simple and seamless, helping you build wealth over time with minimal effort.

3. **Robo-Advisors:** Robo-advisors, such as Betterment and Wealthfront, offer automated investment management based on algorithms and data analysis. These platforms provide personalized investment portfolios, automatic rebalancing, and tax-efficient strategies at a fraction of the cost of traditional financial advisors. Robo-advisors are ideal for investors seeking a low-cost, hands-off approach to investing, with the added benefit of diversification and professional management.

4. **Personal Finance Aggregators:** Personal finance aggregators, like Personal Capital, allow you to view all your financial accounts in one place. These platforms provide a comprehensive overview of your net worth, investment performance, and retirement planning. By consolidating your financial information, you can gain insights into your overall financial health and make informed decisions about your investments and savings.

Using Financial Tools for Investment Management

Investment management tools can help you optimize your portfolio, track performance, and make data-driven decisions. Here's how to use these tools effectively:

1. **Investment Tracking Apps:** Apps like Robinhood, E*TRADE, and Charles Schwab offer features for tracking and managing your investments. These platforms provide real-time market data, research tools, and trading capabilities, allowing you to stay informed about market trends and execute trades efficiently. Many investment tracking apps also offer educational resources and insights to help you make informed investment decisions.
2. **Portfolio Management Software:** Portfolio management software, such as Morningstar or Tiller, helps you analyze and manage your investment portfolio. These tools provide performance reports, asset allocation analysis, and risk assessments, enabling you to track your portfolio's performance and make adjustments as needed. By using portfolio management software, you can ensure your investments align with your financial goals and risk tolerance.
3. **Financial Planning Platforms:** Financial planning platforms, like SmartAdvisor and eMoney, offer comprehensive tools for creating and managing financial plans. These platforms provide features for budgeting, retirement planning, and goal setting, helping you develop a detailed financial plan and track your progress. Financial planning platforms often include scenario analysis and

forecasting tools, allowing you to model different financial outcomes and make informed decisions.

4. **Tax Optimization Tools**: Tax optimization tools, such as TurboTax and H&R Block, assist in preparing and filing your taxes efficiently. These tools offer features for maximizing deductions, credits, and tax-saving opportunities, ensuring you minimize your tax liability. By using tax optimization tools, you can streamline the tax preparation process and ensure compliance with tax regulations.

Integrating Fintech Tools into Your Financial Strategy

To effectively integrate fintech tools into your financial strategy, consider the following steps:

1. **Assess Your Needs**: Evaluate your financial goals, challenges, and preferences to determine which fintech tools and platforms best meet your needs. Whether you're looking for budgeting solutions, investment management, or tax optimization, choose tools that align with your financial objectives and provide the features you require.
2. **Stay Informed**: Keep up-to-date with the latest fintech developments and innovations. The fintech landscape is constantly evolving, with new tools and platforms emerging regularly. Staying informed about new technologies can help you identify opportunities to enhance your financial strategy and make the most of available resources.

3. **Ensure Security**: When using fintech tools, prioritize security and privacy. Choose platforms with strong security measures, such as encryption and multi-factor authentication, to protect your financial information. Regularly review security settings and stay vigilant against potential threats.

In summary, leveraging financial technology and tools can greatly enhance your financial planning and investment management. By embracing fintech innovations, using investment management tools, and integrating these resources into your strategy, you can optimize your financial approach and achieve your financial goals more effectively. In the next chapter, we'll explore the role of financial education and continuous learning in maintaining financial success and adapting to evolving financial landscapes.

Continuing from our exploration of financial technology (fintech) and tools, the second half of this chapter will focus on how to leverage these resources for long-term financial success, integrate them effectively into your strategy, and continuously adapt to technological advancements. By understanding and applying these principles, you can maximize the benefits of fintech and enhance your overall financial management.

Enhancing Long-Term Financial Success

Leveraging fintech tools can significantly contribute to long-term financial success by providing better insights, improving efficiency, and enabling more informed decision-making. Here's how you can use these tools to achieve sustained financial growth:

1. **Enhanced Financial Insights**: Financial technology offers advanced analytics and reporting features that provide deep insights into your financial health. Platforms like Personal Capital and Mint offer comprehensive views of your net worth, spending patterns, and investment performance. By regularly reviewing these insights, you can identify trends, assess your financial progress, and make strategic adjustments to stay on track with your goals.

2. **Optimized Investment Strategies**: Utilizing fintech tools for investment management can enhance your investment strategies and improve your returns. Robo-advisors and investment tracking apps provide real-time market data, portfolio analysis, and automatic rebalancing. By leveraging these tools, you can stay informed about market trends, manage risk more effectively, and make data-driven decisions to optimize your investment portfolio.

3. **Streamlined Financial Planning**: Financial planning platforms help streamline the process of creating and managing a comprehensive financial plan. Tools like eMoney and SmartAdvisor offer features for budgeting, retirement planning, and goal setting. By using these platforms, you can develop a detailed financial plan, track

your progress, and adjust your strategies as needed to achieve your long-term objectives.

4. **Efficient Tax Management:** Tax optimization tools play a crucial role in managing your tax liabilities and maximizing deductions. Platforms like TurboTax and H&R Block provide user-friendly interfaces for preparing and filing taxes, while also offering features to identify tax-saving opportunities. By integrating these tools into your financial strategy, you can ensure compliance, reduce your tax burden, and enhance overall financial efficiency.

Integrating Fintech Tools into Your Financial Strategy

To effectively integrate fintech tools into your financial strategy, consider the following steps:

1. **Develop a Comprehensive Strategy:** Create a comprehensive strategy that incorporates various fintech tools to address different aspects of your financial management. For instance, use budgeting apps to track daily expenses, robo-advisors for investment management, and tax optimization tools for tax planning. Ensure that these tools work together seamlessly to support your overall financial goals.

2. **Set Clear Objectives:** Define clear financial objectives and align your fintech tool usage with these goals. Whether you aim to save for retirement, manage debt, or grow your investment portfolio, ensure that the tools you choose help you achieve these objectives

effectively. Regularly review your goals and adjust your tool usage as needed to stay aligned with your evolving needs.

3. **Monitor and Evaluate**: Continuously monitor and evaluate the performance of the fintech tools you use. Assess their effectiveness in meeting your financial needs and providing value. Solicit feedback from other users, read reviews, and stay informed about updates and new features to ensure that you are utilizing the best tools available.

4. **Adapt to Technological Advancements**: The fintech landscape is constantly evolving, with new technologies and tools emerging regularly. Stay informed about the latest advancements and consider adopting new tools that offer enhanced features or capabilities. Embracing technological innovations can help you stay ahead in financial management and capitalize on emerging opportunities.

5. **Ensure Security and Privacy**: Prioritize security and privacy when using fintech tools. Choose platforms with robust security measures, such as encryption and multi-factor authentication, to protect your financial information. Regularly review security settings and stay vigilant against potential threats to safeguard your data.

Continuous Learning and Adaptation

Financial technology is a dynamic field, and continuous learning is essential to maximize its benefits. Engage in ongoing education to stay updated on fintech trends, tools, and best practices. Participate in webinars, read industry blogs, and explore educational resources to deepen your understanding and make informed decisions.

In conclusion, leveraging fintech tools can greatly enhance your financial management, investment strategies, and overall success. By integrating these tools effectively into your financial strategy, monitoring their performance, and staying adaptable to technological advancements, you can optimize your financial approach and achieve long-term growth. In the next chapter, we'll explore the role of financial education in maintaining financial success and adapting to changing financial landscapes.

Chapter 8: Financial Education for Sustaining Success

Financial education is more than just a prerequisite for achieving initial financial success; it is a continuous journey that plays a critical role in maintaining and expanding your wealth over time. In this chapter, we will explore the importance of financial education, how to develop and enhance your financial knowledge, and how to apply this knowledge to sustain and grow your financial success.

The Importance of Financial Education

Financial education provides the foundation for making informed and strategic financial decisions. It equips you with the knowledge and skills needed to navigate complex financial landscapes, understand investment opportunities, and manage risks effectively. Here's why financial education is crucial for sustaining success:

1. **Informed Decision-Making**: With a solid understanding of financial principles, you can make informed decisions regarding investments, budgeting, and financial planning. Financial education helps you analyze various options, weigh the potential risks and rewards, and choose strategies that align with your long-term goals.

2. **Adaptation to Market Changes**: Financial markets and economic conditions are constantly evolving. Staying educated about market trends, new financial products, and

regulatory changes allows you to adapt your strategies and make timely adjustments to your portfolio. This adaptability is essential for maintaining financial success in a dynamic environment.

3. **Effective Risk Management:** Understanding financial concepts such as diversification, asset allocation, and risk management is key to protecting your wealth. Financial education helps you identify and mitigate potential risks, ensuring that your investments are well-positioned to withstand market fluctuations and economic uncertainties.

4. **Avoiding Common Pitfalls:** Financial education provides insights into common pitfalls and mistakes that investors and individuals often encounter. By learning from these pitfalls and understanding the underlying principles, you can avoid costly errors and make better financial decisions.

Developing and Enhancing Financial Knowledge

Building and enhancing your financial knowledge is an ongoing process. Here are some strategies to develop a strong foundation in financial education:

1. **Formal Education and Certifications:** Consider pursuing formal education or certifications in finance, accounting, or investment management. Programs such as Certified Financial Planner (CFP), Chartered Financial

Analyst (CFA), or even online courses can provide in-depth knowledge and credentials that enhance your expertise.

2. **Reading and Research:** Regularly read books, articles, and research papers on finance, investing, and economic trends. Authors like Benjamin Graham, Warren Buffett, and other financial experts offer valuable insights and strategies that can deepen your understanding. Stay updated with industry publications and financial news to keep abreast of current developments.

3. **Attending Workshops and Seminars:** Participate in workshops, seminars, and webinars focused on financial topics. These events offer opportunities to learn from industry experts, network with peers, and gain practical insights into financial management and investment strategies.

4. **Utilizing Online Resources:** Take advantage of online resources, such as financial blogs, podcasts, and educational websites. Platforms like Investopedia, Khan Academy, and Coursera offer valuable information and courses on various financial topics. Engage with online communities and forums to exchange ideas and learn from others' experiences.

5. **Working with Financial Advisors:** Collaborate with financial advisors or mentors who can provide personalized guidance and support. Financial advisors offer expertise and experience that can help you navigate complex financial situations and refine your strategies. Seek advisors with relevant credentials and a track record of success.

Applying Financial Education to Sustain Success

Once you've developed a strong foundation in financial education, applying this knowledge effectively is crucial for sustaining and growing your financial success. Here's how to apply your financial education:

1. **Implementing Strategies**: Use your financial knowledge to implement and manage strategies that align with your goals. Whether it's optimizing your investment portfolio, creating a comprehensive financial plan, or managing debt, apply the principles you've learned to achieve desired outcomes.
2. **Regular Reviews and Adjustments**: Conduct regular reviews of your financial strategies and performance. Assess the effectiveness of your investments, budget, and financial plans. Use your knowledge to make necessary adjustments and refine your approach based on changing circumstances and new information.
3. **Continuous Learning**: Commit to continuous learning and staying updated with the latest financial trends and developments. Financial education is not a one-time endeavor but an ongoing process. Embrace new information, adapt your strategies, and remain proactive in enhancing your financial knowledge.

In summary, financial education is a vital component of sustaining and expanding your financial success. By developing and enhancing your financial knowledge and applying it effectively, you can make informed decisions, manage risks, and adapt to changing conditions. In the next chapter, we'll explore how to cultivate a mindset for financial success and leverage psychological principles to achieve your financial goals.

Now let's delve into the practical application of financial education in your everyday life. We will discuss how to integrate financial knowledge into your decision-making processes, create a culture of financial literacy in your personal and professional life, and leverage psychological principles to enhance financial success.

Integrating Financial Knowledge into Decision-Making

Applying your financial education to everyday decision-making is crucial for maximizing your financial outcomes. Here's how to effectively integrate financial knowledge into your decisions:

1. **Strategic Financial Planning**: Use your understanding of financial principles to develop a comprehensive financial plan. This plan should encompass your goals, investment strategies, risk management, and budgeting. By aligning your plan with your financial education, you can ensure that your strategies are well-informed and targeted towards achieving long-term success.

2. **Evaluating Investment Opportunities:** When assessing potential investments, apply the concepts and techniques you've learned to evaluate their viability. Analyze factors such as risk, return, market conditions, and alignment with your financial goals. Utilize financial metrics and valuation techniques to make informed investment decisions and optimize your portfolio.
3. **Budgeting and Expense Management:** Implement effective budgeting techniques to manage your expenses and savings. Use your knowledge to create a budget that aligns with your financial goals, tracks your spending, and identifies areas for improvement. Regularly review and adjust your budget based on changes in income, expenses, and financial objectives.
4. **Tax Planning and Optimization:** Apply tax strategies and optimization techniques to manage your tax liabilities efficiently. Utilize your understanding of tax laws and deductions to minimize your tax burden. Plan for tax-efficient investments and explore opportunities to maximize tax savings through retirement accounts and charitable contributions.

Creating a Culture of Financial Literacy

Fostering a culture of financial literacy within your personal and professional circles can amplify the impact of your financial education. Here's how to create and promote financial literacy:

1. **Educating Family and Friends:** Share your financial knowledge with family and friends to help them improve their financial literacy. Discuss key concepts, offer guidance on budgeting and investing, and provide resources for further learning. Encouraging financial education within your personal network can lead to better financial decisions and improved financial well-being for everyone involved.
2. **Promoting Financial Literacy in the Workplace:** Advocate for financial literacy programs and resources in your workplace. Support initiatives such as workshops, seminars, and financial counseling for employees. By fostering a culture of financial education at work, you contribute to the overall financial health and productivity of your organization.
3. **Supporting Financial Education Initiatives:** Get involved in community programs and initiatives that promote financial education. Volunteer to teach financial literacy classes, support nonprofit organizations focused on financial education, or contribute to financial education research. Your involvement can help spread financial knowledge and empower others to make informed financial decisions.

Leveraging Psychological Principles for Financial Success

Understanding and applying psychological principles can enhance your financial success by influencing behavior and decision-making. Here's how to leverage psychology to achieve your financial goals:

1. **Mindset and Behavioral Finance:** Develop a growth mindset that embraces continuous learning and improvement. Understand the principles of behavioral finance, such as cognitive biases and emotional influences on decision-making. By recognizing and addressing these biases, you can make more rational and objective financial decisions.
2. **Setting and Achieving Goals:** Use psychological techniques to set and achieve financial goals. Employ strategies such as setting SMART (Specific, Measurable, Achievable, Relevant, Time-bound) goals, breaking goals into smaller milestones, and tracking progress. Visualization and affirmation techniques can also help reinforce your commitment to achieving your goals.
3. **Managing Financial Stress:** Financial stress can impact decision-making and overall well-being. Implement stress management techniques such as mindfulness, relaxation exercises, and time management to reduce financial stress. Maintaining a balanced approach to financial planning and focusing on long-term goals can help mitigate stress and enhance financial stability.
4. **Building Positive Financial Habits:** Cultivate positive financial habits by incorporating behavioral psychology principles. Establish routines, create financial rituals, and use rewards to reinforce good financial behaviors. Building habits such as regular saving, consistent investing, and disciplined spending can lead to long-term financial success.

In summary, integrating financial knowledge into your decision-making, fostering a culture of financial literacy, and applying psychological principles can significantly enhance your financial success. By leveraging your financial education in practical ways and promoting financial literacy, you can sustain and grow your wealth while achieving your financial goals. In the next chapter, we will explore strategies for long-term wealth preservation and succession planning to ensure that your financial success endures for generations to come.

Chapter 9: Strategies for Generational Wealth

Building wealth is only one part of the financial journey; preserving it and ensuring its smooth transition to future generations is equally crucial. This chapter delves into strategies for long-term wealth preservation and effective succession planning, ensuring that your hard-earned assets continue to benefit your family and legacy long after you're gone.

Long-Term Wealth Preservation

Preserving wealth involves strategies and practices designed to protect your assets from erosion due to market fluctuations, inflation, taxes, and other financial risks. Here's how you can ensure your wealth remains intact over the long term:

1. **Diversification:** Diversifying your investment portfolio is a fundamental strategy for mitigating risk. Spread your investments across various asset classes, such as stocks, bonds, real estate, and alternative investments. Diversification helps reduce the impact of poor performance in any single asset class and provides a buffer against market volatility.
2. **Inflation Protection:** Inflation can erode the purchasing power of your wealth over time. To protect against inflation, consider investing in assets that historically outpace inflation, such as real estate, stocks, or

inflation-protected securities. Additionally, incorporating inflation-adjusted income sources, like annuities with cost-of-living adjustments, can help maintain your purchasing power.

3. **Risk Management:** Implement a comprehensive risk management strategy to protect your wealth from unforeseen events. This includes having adequate insurance coverage for health, life, property, and liability. Additionally, consider strategies like estate planning and asset protection trusts to shield your wealth from legal claims or creditor actions.

4. **Regular Reviews and Rebalancing:** Conduct regular reviews of your investment portfolio and financial strategies to ensure they remain aligned with your goals. Periodic rebalancing helps maintain your desired asset allocation and adapt to changing market conditions. Regular reviews also provide an opportunity to adjust your strategies based on life events or financial changes.

5. **Tax Efficiency:** Employ tax-efficient strategies to minimize your tax liabilities and maximize your after-tax returns. This includes utilizing tax-advantaged accounts, such as IRAs or 401(k)s, and taking advantage of deductions, credits, and tax-loss harvesting. Work with a tax professional to develop a strategy that optimizes your tax situation and preserves your wealth.

Succession Planning

Succession planning ensures that your assets are distributed according to your wishes and that your legacy is preserved for future generations. Effective succession planning involves several key components:

1. **Creating a Will:** A will is a fundamental element of succession planning. It outlines how your assets will be distributed upon your death and designates guardians for minor children. Ensure that your will is legally valid, up-to-date, and reflects your current wishes. Regularly review and update your will to account for changes in your financial situation or family dynamics.
2. **Establishing Trusts:** Trusts offer additional flexibility and control over how your assets are distributed. Revocable living trusts allow you to retain control over your assets during your lifetime and provide for a seamless transition upon your death. Irrevocable trusts can offer tax benefits and protection from creditors. Work with an estate planning attorney to determine the most appropriate type of trust for your needs.
3. **Designating Beneficiaries:** Review and update beneficiary designations on accounts such as life insurance policies, retirement accounts, and investment accounts. Beneficiary designations supersede provisions in a will or trust, so ensure that they are current and align with your overall estate plan.
4. **Planning for Incapacity:** Succession planning also involves preparing for potential incapacity. Establishing powers of attorney for financial and healthcare decisions

ensures that someone you trust can manage your affairs and make decisions on your behalf if you become unable to do so. Clearly communicate your preferences and wishes to your chosen agents.

5. **Family Communication:** Open and honest communication with family members about your succession plans is vital. Discussing your plans can prevent misunderstandings and conflicts among heirs. Ensure that your family understands your wishes and the rationale behind your decisions, fostering a smooth transition and preserving family harmony.

In summary, long-term wealth preservation and effective succession planning are essential for maintaining and transferring your financial legacy. By implementing strategies for diversification, risk management, and tax efficiency, and by developing a comprehensive succession plan, you can protect your assets and ensure your legacy endures for future generations. In the second half of this chapter, we will explore how to implement these strategies in practice and address common challenges associated with wealth preservation and succession planning.

For the rest of this chapter I will explain some tips on the practical implementation of wealth preservation and succession planning strategies. We'll address common challenges and provide actionable steps to ensure your financial legacy is managed effectively and efficiently.

Implementing Wealth Preservation Strategies

Successfully implementing wealth preservation strategies requires careful planning and execution. Here's how to put these strategies into practice:

1. **Building a Diversified Portfolio**: To effectively diversify your investment portfolio, start by assessing your current asset allocation. Ensure you have exposure to a variety of asset classes, including domestic and international stocks, bonds, real estate, and alternative investments such as commodities or private equity. Utilize low-cost index funds or exchange-traded funds (ETFs) to achieve broad diversification with minimal expense. Regularly review and adjust your portfolio to maintain the desired allocation and respond to market changes.
2. **Inflation Protection Tactics**: Incorporate inflation-protected securities, such as Treasury Inflation-Protected Securities (TIPS), into your investment strategy. These securities adjust with inflation, helping to preserve your purchasing power. Additionally, consider investing in real estate properties or real estate investment trusts (REITs), which historically have provided a hedge against inflation. Regularly review your investment mix to ensure it includes assets that are likely to outperform inflation.
3. **Implementing Risk Management**: Review your insurance policies to ensure they provide adequate coverage for your assets and liabilities. This includes health, life,

disability, and property insurance. Consider working with a risk management advisor to identify potential vulnerabilities and recommend additional coverage if necessary. To protect your estate from potential legal claims, explore options such as establishing asset protection trusts or incorporating insurance products like umbrella liability policies.

4. **Enhancing Tax Efficiency**: Utilize tax-advantaged accounts like Roth IRAs, 401(k)s, and health savings accounts (HSAs) to defer or eliminate taxes on your investments. Employ tax-loss harvesting strategies to offset capital gains with investment losses. Work with a tax advisor to create a tax-efficient withdrawal strategy during retirement, ensuring you minimize your tax liabilities while maximizing your retirement income.

Executing Effective Succession Planning

Effective succession planning involves creating a clear and actionable plan to manage your estate and legacy. Here's how to implement these plans effectively:

1. **Drafting and Updating Legal Documents**: Work with an estate planning attorney to draft a will and establish trusts. Ensure that these documents reflect your current wishes and address key aspects such as asset distribution, guardianship of minor children, and medical decisions. Regularly review and update these documents to

account for changes in your financial situation, family dynamics, or legal requirements.

2. **Establishing and Managing Trusts**: When setting up trusts, select a reliable trustee who will manage the trust assets according to your wishes. Clearly outline the terms and conditions of the trust in the trust agreement, including how assets should be distributed and any specific instructions for the trustee. Periodically review the trust's performance and ensure it continues to meet your objectives.

3. **Updating Beneficiary Designations**: Regularly review beneficiary designations on accounts such as life insurance policies, retirement accounts, and investment accounts. Ensure that these designations align with your overall estate plan and update them as needed to reflect changes in your personal circumstances or financial goals.

4. **Planning for Incapacity**: Create durable powers of attorney for both financial and healthcare decisions. Choose trusted individuals who will act in your best interests if you become incapacitated. Clearly document your preferences for medical treatment and financial management, and discuss these preferences with your chosen agents to ensure they are prepared to make informed decisions on your behalf.

5. **Facilitating Family Discussions**: Engage in open and honest discussions with your family about your succession plan. Explain your decisions, the rationale behind them, and how you envision the transition process. Providing

clear communication can help prevent conflicts and ensure that your wishes are respected. Consider holding family meetings with an estate planning professional to address any questions or concerns.

Addressing Common Challenges

Several challenges can arise during the process of wealth preservation and succession planning. Address these challenges proactively to ensure a smooth and effective plan:

1.   **Family Disagreements**: Conflicts among family members can arise when dealing with estate planning and asset distribution. Address potential issues early by having open discussions and seeking mediation if necessary. Clear documentation and communication can help mitigate misunderstandings and disputes.
2.   **Changing Laws and Regulations**: Tax laws, estate planning regulations, and financial regulations can change over time. Stay informed about relevant legal changes and consult with professionals to adjust your plan accordingly. Regularly review and update your strategies to ensure compliance and alignment with current laws.
3.   **Emotional Considerations**: Estate planning and wealth preservation can involve emotional aspects, particularly when addressing sensitive family dynamics. Approach these discussions with empathy and sensitivity.

Seek professional guidance to help navigate complex emotional and financial issues.

In summary, implementing effective wealth preservation and succession planning strategies involves careful execution, regular review, and proactive management. By addressing common challenges and applying practical steps, you can ensure that your financial legacy is well-preserved and successfully passed on to future generations. In the final chapter, we'll explore how to continuously adapt and evolve your financial strategies to stay aligned with your goals and the ever-changing financial landscape.

Chapter 10: Adapting to the Evolving Financial Landscape

As the financial world evolves, staying ahead of trends and adapting your strategies is crucial for maintaining and growing your wealth. In this chapter, we'll explore how to navigate changes in the financial landscape, leverage emerging opportunities, and continuously refine your financial strategies to ensure long-term success.

Understanding Financial Trends and Changes

The financial landscape is constantly shifting due to technological advancements, economic developments, regulatory changes, and market dynamics. Understanding these trends is essential for making informed decisions and adapting your strategies effectively. Here are key areas to focus on:

1. **Technological Advancements**: Financial technology (fintech) is rapidly transforming the industry. Innovations such as blockchain, artificial intelligence (AI), and robo-advisors are reshaping how financial services are delivered and managed. Stay informed about these technologies and assess how they can enhance your investment strategies, improve financial management, and provide new opportunities. For example, blockchain technology can offer greater transparency and security in transactions, while AI-driven tools can provide

personalized investment recommendations and risk assessments.

2. **Economic Developments**: Global and local economic conditions significantly impact financial markets and investment opportunities. Monitor economic indicators such as interest rates, inflation, and employment rates, as well as geopolitical events and trade policies. These factors influence market performance and can create opportunities or risks for investors. Stay updated with economic reports, analyses, and forecasts to make timely and informed decisions.

3. **Regulatory Changes**: Financial regulations and tax laws are subject to change, which can affect your investment strategies, tax liabilities, and estate planning. Keep abreast of regulatory updates and work with financial professionals to ensure compliance and optimize your strategies. For instance, changes in tax laws may impact your investment decisions or require adjustments to your estate plan.

4. **Market Dynamics**: Financial markets are influenced by various factors, including market cycles, investor sentiment, and sector performance. Understand market trends and cycles to make strategic adjustments to your portfolio. For example, during a market downturn, consider defensive investment strategies or opportunities in undervalued assets. Conversely, in a bullish market, explore growth opportunities and emerging sectors.

Leveraging Emerging Opportunities

Adapting to the evolving financial landscape involves not only responding to changes but also proactively seeking and leveraging new opportunities. Here's how to identify and capitalize on emerging trends:

1. **Identifying Growth Sectors**: Emerging sectors such as renewable energy, technology, and biotechnology present significant growth opportunities. Research and analyze these sectors to identify promising investments. Consider factors such as market potential, innovation, and regulatory support. Investing in growth sectors can provide substantial returns and diversify your portfolio.
2. **Exploring Alternative Investments**: Alternative investments, including private equity, venture capital, and cryptocurrencies, offer unique opportunities for diversification and potential high returns. Evaluate the risks and benefits associated with these investments and consider incorporating them into your portfolio as part of a broader strategy. Due diligence and professional guidance are crucial when exploring alternative investments.
3. **Adopting Sustainable and Responsible Investing**: Environmental, social, and governance (ESG) factors are becoming increasingly important in investment decisions. Sustainable and responsible investing focuses on companies and projects that align with ethical and environmental standards. Incorporate ESG criteria into your investment strategy to support positive societal impacts and potentially benefit from growing investor interest in sustainable investments.

4. **Utilizing Data and Analytics**: Advanced data analytics and big data provide valuable insights for making informed financial decisions. Leverage data-driven tools and platforms to analyze market trends, assess investment opportunities, and track your financial performance. Data analytics can enhance your ability to make strategic decisions and respond to changing market conditions.

Continuous Refinement of Financial Strategies

Adapting to the evolving financial landscape requires continuous refinement of your strategies. Here's how to maintain flexibility and ensure your strategies remain effective:

1. **Regular Reviews and Adjustments**: Periodically review your financial strategies, investment portfolio, and financial goals. Assess performance against benchmarks and make adjustments based on changes in market conditions, economic developments, or personal circumstances. Regular reviews ensure that your strategies remain aligned with your objectives and risk tolerance.
2. **Embracing Lifelong Learning**: Stay informed about financial trends, new technologies, and investment opportunities through ongoing education. Attend workshops, read industry publications, and engage with financial experts to expand your knowledge and stay ahead of developments. Lifelong learning equips you with the

insights needed to adapt and thrive in a dynamic financial environment.

3. **Seeking Professional Guidance:** Collaborate with financial advisors, tax professionals, and estate planners to receive expert advice and guidance. Professionals can provide valuable insights, recommend strategies, and help you navigate complex financial situations. Building a team of trusted advisors ensures that you have the support needed to adapt to changes and achieve your financial goals.

In summary, adapting to the evolving financial landscape involves understanding trends, leveraging emerging opportunities, and continuously refining your strategies. By staying informed, embracing new technologies, and seeking professional guidance, you can navigate changes effectively and ensure long-term financial success.

As we continue our exploration of adapting to the evolving financial landscape, the focus shifts to implementing practical steps for effective adaptation and managing transitions to new financial approaches. This section provides actionable strategies to ensure your financial plans remain relevant and resilient amidst ongoing changes.

Implementing Adaptation Strategies

Adapting to a shifting financial environment involves more than just awareness; it requires proactive measures and strategic adjustments. Here's how to effectively implement adaptation strategies:

1. **Developing a Flexible Financial Plan:** Create a financial plan that incorporates flexibility to accommodate changing circumstances. Build contingencies into your plan to address potential market fluctuations, economic shifts, or personal changes. For example, include alternative investment options or emergency funds to cushion against unexpected events. A flexible plan allows you to adjust your strategies without compromising your long-term goals.

2. **Incorporating Technology into Financial Management:** Leverage financial technology tools to enhance your financial management. Utilize budgeting apps, investment tracking platforms, and financial planning software to streamline your processes and gain real-time insights. These tools can help you monitor your portfolio, track expenses, and make informed decisions based on up-to-date information. Embracing technology can also improve efficiency and accuracy in managing your finances.

3. **Setting Up Regular Financial Check-Ins:** Establish a routine for regular financial check-ins to review your progress and make necessary adjustments. Schedule periodic meetings with your financial advisor to assess your portfolio performance, evaluate your financial goals, and discuss potential changes. These check-ins provide an

opportunity to stay aligned with your objectives and adapt to any emerging trends or challenges.

4. **Building a Resilient Investment Portfolio:** Construct an investment portfolio designed to withstand market volatility and economic downturns. Include a mix of asset classes, such as equities, bonds, real estate, and alternative investments, to diversify risk. Consider incorporating low-volatility or defensive stocks during uncertain times. A resilient portfolio helps safeguard your wealth and ensures stability during market fluctuations.

5. **Enhancing Risk Management Practices:** Strengthen your risk management strategies to protect your assets from potential threats. Evaluate and adjust your insurance coverage to address new risks or changes in your financial situation. Implement strategies like hedging or diversification to mitigate exposure to specific risks. A comprehensive risk management approach enhances your ability to navigate uncertainties and safeguard your financial health.

Managing Transitions to New Financial Approaches

Transitioning to new financial approaches involves careful planning and execution. Here's how to manage these transitions effectively:

1. **Gradual Implementation of New Strategies:** When adopting new financial strategies or technologies, consider implementing them gradually. Start with smaller

investments or pilot projects to test their effectiveness before fully committing. This phased approach allows you to evaluate the impact and make adjustments as needed. Gradual implementation reduces the risk of disruptions and ensures a smoother transition.

2. **Communicating Changes to Stakeholders:** If you are managing investments or financial strategies that impact others, such as family members or business partners, communicate any changes clearly and transparently. Explain the reasons for the adjustments, the expected outcomes, and how they may affect stakeholders. Open communication helps manage expectations and fosters collaboration during the transition.

3. **Evaluating and Adapting New Technologies:** When incorporating new technologies into your financial management, assess their compatibility with your existing systems and processes. Evaluate their effectiveness and user experience to ensure they meet your needs. Stay informed about updates and advancements in financial technology to continuously optimize your tools and leverage the latest innovations.

4. **Training and Skill Development:** Invest in training and skill development to effectively use new financial tools and strategies. Attend workshops, webinars, or courses to gain proficiency in emerging technologies or investment approaches. Building your expertise enhances your ability to implement new strategies successfully and adapt to evolving trends.

5. **Monitoring and Adjusting Transition Processes:** Continuously monitor the transition process and assess its impact on your financial objectives. Track key performance indicators and gather feedback to evaluate the effectiveness of the new approaches. Be prepared to make adjustments based on performance data and evolving circumstances. Monitoring and adjusting ensure that your transition remains on track and aligned with your goals.

Embracing Continuous Improvement

Adapting to the evolving financial landscape is an ongoing process that requires continuous improvement. Here's how to embrace a mindset of continuous improvement:

1. **Cultivating a Growth Mindset:** Adopt a growth mindset that values learning and adaptation. Embrace change as an opportunity for growth and improvement. Be open to experimenting with new approaches and technologies, and view challenges as chances to refine your strategies and enhance your financial management.
2. **Seeking Feedback and Insights:** Actively seek feedback from financial advisors, peers, and industry experts. Engage in discussions and networks to gain diverse perspectives and insights. Feedback and insights can provide valuable information for refining your strategies and staying ahead of trends.
3. **Staying Informed and Educated:** Commit to lifelong learning and staying informed about financial trends and

developments. Read industry publications, attend conferences, and engage in educational opportunities to expand your knowledge. Staying educated ensures you remain proactive and well-prepared to adapt to changes.

In summary, adapting to the evolving financial landscape requires practical implementation of strategies, careful management of transitions, and a commitment to continuous improvement. By developing flexible plans, leveraging technology, and staying informed, you can navigate changes effectively and maintain financial success. In conclusion, the key to thriving in an ever-changing financial world lies in your ability to adapt, innovate, and continuously refine your approaches.

Conclusion

Transforming your mental beliefs around money can profoundly upgrade your entire life. Shifting from a scarcity mindset to an abundance mindset not only changes how you perceive financial opportunities but also redefines your entire approach to wealth. By embracing the belief that there is more than enough wealth to go around, you open yourself up to new possibilities and avenues for financial success. This shift in perspective has the power to break down the barriers that once held you back and pave the way for transformative changes in every aspect of your life.

Financial freedom, once an abstract concept, becomes a tangible reality when you embrace an abundance mindset. It liberates you from the constraints of the traditional 9-5 job and the monotonous rat race, allowing you to design a life on your own terms. With financial independence, you can pursue passions, explore new ventures, and enjoy a lifestyle that aligns with your values and aspirations. The freedom to make choices based on what truly matters to you, rather than what's financially necessary, opens up a world of opportunities and fulfillment.

Furthermore, achieving financial freedom provides a secure foundation for your current and future family. It empowers you to provide for your children's education, support their dreams, and ensure a comfortable and prosperous future for them. Knowing that you have the resources to give your children the opportunities they deserve is a powerful motivation and a testament to the transformative impact of financial freedom. By breaking free from financial limitations and cultivating an abundance mindset, you not only enhance your own life but also set the stage for a brighter, more secure future for those you care about.

Printed in Great Britain
by Amazon